Ultimate AAU & College Recruiting Handbook

Copyright © 2025
BY: **C. Grooms & Bobby May**
All rights reserved.

No part of this publication may be reproduced, stored in a retrieval system, or transmitted in any form or by any means which includes electronic, mechanical, photocopying, recording, or otherwise without the prior written permission of the publisher and authors, except in the case of brief quotations embodied in critical articles or reviews.

For information or permissions, contact:
Ten G Publishing
New York, New York
info@tengpublishing.com

All facts and information are presented accurately to the best of the authors' knowledge.
ISBN: 978-1-7359172-4-5

First Edition
Printed in the United States of America

# Ultimate AAU & College Recruiting Handbook

## TABLE OF CONTENTS

| | |
|---|---|
| Module 1 (Understanding The Recruitment Process) | 4 |
| Module 2 (Getting Noticed By College Coaches) | 9 |
| Coach Outreach Template | 13 |
| Module 3 (How To Land A Scholarship And Secure Offers) | 14 |
| The Reality of Athletic Aid | 15 |
| Module 4 (The NIL Playbook: Earning Money Before College) | 19 |
| Module 5 (The Final Recruiting Action Plan) | 26 |
| Beyond The Scholarship | 32 |
| Life After College Athletics | 35 |
| Bonus Content | 38 |
| Article: The Billion Dollar Pipeline | 42 |
| Article: The Real Recruitment Game | 47 |
| Article: Brotherhood Beyond Blood | 52 |
| Article: Teaching Young People To Make Hard Choices | 55 |
| Article: The Geography of Dreams | 58 |
| About The Authors | 61 |

**Ultimate AAU & College Recruiting Playbook**
A Step-by-Step Guide to Navigating AAU, College Recruitment, and NIL Deals

**MODULE 1: UNDERSTANDING THE RECRUITING PROCESS**
**LESSON 1: HOW COLLEGE RECRUITING WORKS**
**NCAA Division I**
- Highest level of collegiate competition
- 351 D1 schools across the United States
- Offers the most athletic scholarships (full rides possible)
- Most competitive level with rigorous time commitments
- Typically recruiting athletes earlier in high school

**Example Schools:** Duke, Kentucky, UCLA, Michigan, Alabama

**NCAA Division II**
- 308 D2 schools nationwide
- Balance between competitive athletics and academics
- Partial scholarships available (often combined with academic aid)
- Less pressure than D1 but still highly competitive
- Strong regional competition focus

**Example Schools:** UC San Diego, Queens University, West Texas A&M

**NCAA Division III**
- Largest NCAA division with 443 schools
- No athletic scholarships offered
- Strong focus on academics over athletics
- Typically less travel and time commitment
- Many prestigious academic institutions

**Example Schools:** MIT, Johns Hopkins, Williams College, Amherst

**NAIA**
- 250+ smaller private institutions
- More flexible recruiting rules than NCAA
- Athletic scholarships available
- Often overlooked but quality competition
- Lower exposure but strong opportunity for playing time

**Example Schools:** Oklahoma City University, Columbia College, Southeastern University

**Junior Colleges (JUCO)**
- Two-year programs across the country
- Excellent option for academic/athletic development
- Athletic scholarships available
- Pathway to transfer to 4-year schools
- Great for late bloomers or academic improvements

**Example Schools:** Indian Hills, Hutchinson CC, Chipola College

## The Recruiting Timeline

### Freshman Year (9th Grade)
- Focus on academics and establishing GPA
- Develop athletic skills and fundamentals
- Research colleges you might be interested in
- Start understanding NCAA eligibility requirements
- Build relationships with high school and club coaches

### Sophomore Year (10th Grade)
- Continuing academic excellence
- Take PSAT/pre-ACT tests
- Begin attending showcases and camps
- Start creating highlight videos
- Register with NCAA Eligibility Center

### Junior Year (11th Grade)
- Critical year for recruitment
- Take SAT/ACT exams
- Develop recruiting profile and videos
- Actively reach out to college coaches
- Visiting campuses unofficially
- Competing in high-visibility tournaments
- Narrow school choices based on fit

### Senior Year (12th Grade)
- Take official visits to top choice schools
- Finalize SAT/ACT scores
- Maintain academic standards
- Make final decision on college choice
- Sign National Letter of Intent (if applicable)
- Apply for scholarships and financial aid

## NCAA Eligibility Requirements

### Academic Requirements:
- Graduate from high school
- Complete 16 NCAA-approved core courses:
- 4 years of English
- 3 years of math (Algebra 1 or higher)
- 2 years of natural/physical science
- 2 years of social science
- 4 years of additional courses (any above, foreign language or religion/philosophy)
- Earning a minimum GPA in core courses
- Sliding scale relationship between GPA and test scores

**Amateurism Requirements:**
- Must maintain amateur status
- Cannot accept payment for playing sports
- Cannot sign with professional agents (with NIL exceptions)
- Cannot try out or practice with professional teams beyond permitted guidelines

**Recruiting Rules and Contact Periods**

**Quiet Period:**
- Coaches can only have in-person contact on campus
- Phone calls and written communication allowed

**Contact Period:**
- Coaches can meet with prospects and parents off-campus
- In-home visits permitted
- Communication via all methods allowed

**Dead Period:**
- No in-person contact allowed on or off campus
- Phone calls and written communication are still permitted

**Evaluation Period:**
- Coaches can watch athletes compete
- No in-person contact off-campus
- Campus visits and phone calls allowed

## LESSON 2: NAVIGATING THE RECRUITMENT JOURNEY
### Self-Assessment: Are You College Material?

**Athletic Assessment:**
- Be honest about your skill level compared to current college athletes
- Get feedback from coaches who understand college requirements
- Analyze your statistics versus college roster players
- Consider your physical development potential
- Evaluate your game against higher-level competition

**Academic Assessment:**
- Review your current GPA versus college requirements
- Understand test score expectations
- Evaluate your study habits and time management
- Consider the academic rigor of target schools
- Be realistic about balancing academics and athletics

**Personal Assessment:**
- Are you prepared to live away from home?
- Can you handle independent responsibility?
- How do you respond to coaching and criticism?
- Are you ready for the increased competition?
- Do you have the work ethic required?

**Finding Your Perfect Fit Athletic Fit:**
- Playing time opportunities
- Coaching style compatibility
- Program culture and values
- Level of competition appropriate for your skills
- Development opportunities

**Academic Fit:**
- Majors and programs available
- Academic support for athletes
- Class sizes and teaching approach
- Graduation rates for athletes
- Career placement success

**Social/Personal Fit:**
- Campus size and location
- Distance from home
- Student body demographics
- Religious or cultural considerations
- Living arrangements and housing options

## The Role of AAU/Club Teams in Recruitment

**Benefits of AAU/Club Participation:**
- Exposure to college coaches
- Higher level of competition
- Year-round skill development
- Tournament and showcase opportunities
- Coaching connections to college programs

**Selecting the Right AAU/Club Program:**
- Coach reputation and college connections
- Tournament schedule and exposure events
- Development focus versus winning focus
- Track record of college placements
- Financial considerations and travel requirements

**Maximizing AAU/Club Exposure:**
- Build relationships with your club coach
- Understand your role on the team
- Perform well in showcase tournaments
- Take advantage of networking opportunities
- Be coachable and demonstrate high character

## Quick Check: Module 1- Understanding the Recruiting Process

1. List one action a student-athlete should take based on this module.
2. Describe one challenge that athletes face during the recruiting process.
3. Summarize one of the most important stats, rules, or timelines mentioned.
4. Why is understanding the levels of college athletics critical?
5. Name one division and what makes it unique.
6. What's one step families often overlook at this stage?

## MODULE 2: GETTING NOTICED BY COLLEGE COACHES
## LESSON 1: HOW TO GET SCOUTED AT AAU TOURNAMENTS

**Understanding How Coaches Scout Tournaments**

**Coach Scouting Priorities:**
- Specific positions and needs for upcoming classes
- Athletic measurables and physical traits
- Skill proficiency and basketball IQ
- Competitiveness and effort level
- Coachability and body language
- Team chemistry and leadership qualities

**Tournament Scouting Reality:**
- Coaches often watch multiple games simultaneously
- They may only see portions of your games
- First impressions matter significantly
- They watch how you handle adversity
- Consistency is more valuable than single-game brilliance

**Pre-Tournament Preparation**

**Research Attending Coaches:**
- Identify schools attending the tournament
- Research their program needs and style
- Prioritize coaches based on your interest level
- Send pre-tournament emails to target coaches
- Understand which courts/times coaches will likely attend

**Physical Preparation:**
- Peak conditioning for tournament schedule
- Proper nutrition and hydration plan
- Adequate sleep before and during events
- Injury prevention strategies and recovery protocol between games

**Mental Preparation:**
- Visualize successful performances
- Develop a consistent pre-game routine
- Prepare for various game situations
- Set realistic performance goals
- Create a positive mindset strategy

## Standing Out During Competition

**On-Court Performance:**
- Excel in your role - don't force highlights
- Demonstrate high basketball IQ
- Show versatility in your skill set
- Communicate effectively with teammates
- Maintain consistent effort level regardless of score

**Body Language and Attitude:**
- Positive reactions to coaching
- Supportive of teammates
- Resilient after mistakes
- Engaged during timeouts
- Controlled emotions under pressure

**Unique Traits to Showcase:**
- Specialized skills that differentiate you
- Exceptional athleticism or size
- Extraordinary court vision or basketball IQ
- Elite shooting or defensive abilities
- Outstanding leadership qualities

## Post-Tournament Follow-Up

**Coach Communication:**
- Send thank-you emails to coaches who watched
- Provide updated stats from the tournament · Ask for feedback on your performance
- Express continued interest in their program
- Schedule campus visits when appropriate

**Performance Analysis:**
- Review game film to assess your performance
- Identify strengths to emphasize
- Recognize weaknesses to improve
- Compare your play to college-level expectations
- Adjust training based on tournament experience

## LESSON 2: CREATING AN EFFECTIVE RECRUITING PROFILE
Building Your Digital Presence Essential

**Online Profiles:**
- NCSA, Be Recruited, or similar recruiting platforms
- Social media accounts (Instagram, Twitter, LinkedIn)
- Personal website or digital portfolio
- YouTube channel for video content
- MaxPreps or other statistics platforms

**Content Strategy:**
- Consistent posting schedule
- Mix of athletic and academic accomplishments
- Character-demonstrating content
- Community involvement and leadership
- Appropriate, professional presentation

**Managing Your Digital Footprint:**
- Regular audit of all social media
- Privacy settings configuration
- Content appropriateness evaluation
- Strategic use of hashtags and keywords
- Engagement with college program accounts

**Highlight Videos That Get Watched**

**Essential Video Content:**
- Introduction with name, position, graduation year
- Key measurables (height, weight, wingspan, etc.)
- 3-5 minutes of game highlights (not practice)
- Progressive skill demonstration
- Game context (score, time, situation)
- Contact information at end

**Technical Considerations:**
- High-definition video quality
- Proper editing and transitions
- Clear player identification (spotlight or arrow)
- Multiple game footage sources
- Good audio quality or appropriate music

**Distribution Strategy:**
- YouTube or Hudl hosting
- Direct links in coach communications
- Social media promotion
- Recruiting profile integration
- Regular updates with new footage

**Follow-Up Strategy:**
- Email every 2-3 weeks with updates
- Reference previous communications
- Provide new achievements or video
- Ask specific questions about their program
- Gradually build relationship over time

**Campus Visits and Showcases**

**Unofficial Visit Planning:**
- Research program thoroughly beforehand
- Contact coaches to arrange meetings
- Prepare questions for coaches and players
- Tour facilities and campus
- Attend games or practices if possible

**Official Visit Preparation:**
- Understand NCAA rules and limitations
- Know what expenses are covered
- Prepare for in-depth coach meetings
- Plan to interact with current players
- Consider academic department visits

**Camp and Showcase Selection:**
- Prioritize school-specific camps for serious interest
- Research which coaches attend multi-school events
- Consider cost-benefit of each opportunity
- Prepare specifically for the showcase format
- Follow up immediately after attending

## Quick Check: Module 2- Getting Noticed by College Coaches

1. What's one thing that can help a player stand out to a coach?
2. Why does timing matter when reaching out to a college coach?
3. Give an example of something that can hurt a player's chances with recruiters.
4. What role does video footage or social media play in recruiting?
5. What's one misconception players or parents have about visibility?
6. How should an athlete prepare before contacting a coach?

**Direct Coach Outreach**

**Initial Contact Email Template:**
Subject: [Your Name] - [Graduation Year] - [Position] - [Key Stat/Achievement]
Dear Coach [Name],

My name is [Your Name], a [height/weight] [position] from [High School/Club Team] in [City, State].
I'm currently maintaining a [GPA] GPA and will graduate in [Year].
I'm reaching out because I've been following [College Name]'s program and am particularly impressed with [specific aspect of their program].
I believe my [specific skills/playing style] would be a great fit for your system.

Key achievements:
- [Statistic/Achievement 1]
- [Statistic/Achievement 2]
- [Statistic/Achievement 3]

You can view my highlight video here: [Link]
My complete game film is available here: [Link]
My upcoming tournament schedule is:
[Tournament 1] - [Date] - [Location]
[Tournament 2] - [Date] - [Location]

I would appreciate the opportunity to learn more about your program and how I might contribute. I'll be following up with updated performances after my upcoming tournaments.

Thank you for your consideration,
[Your Name]
[Phone Number]
[Email]

## MODULE 3: HOW TO LAND A SCHOLARSHIP & SECURE OFFERS
## LESSON 1: UNDERSTANDING ATHLETIC SCHOLARSHIPS

**Types of Athletic Scholarships Full Scholarships:**
- Cover tuition, fees, room, board, and books
- Primarily available at D1 programs
- Limited to "head count" sports (basketball, football, etc.)
- Highly competitive and limited in number
- Usually reserved for top-tier recruits

**Partial Scholarships:**
- Covers a percentage of college costs
- Common in sports
- Can be combined with academic scholarships
- May increase over time with performance
- Requires careful financial planning for remainder

**Academic/Athletic Combination:**
- Strategic approach for maximizing aid
- Particularly valuable at D3 schools (no athletic scholarships)
- Requires strong GPA and test scores
- Can often exceed value of partial athletic scholarships
- Provides security if athletic career ends prematurely

**Scholarship Limitations by Division**

**Division I:**
- Basketball: 13 scholarships (men), 15 (women)
- Football: 85 scholarships (FBS), 63 (FCS)
- Baseball: 11.7 scholarships (typically split among 27+ players)
- Track & Field: 12.6 (men), 18 (women)
- Soccer: 9.9 (men), 14 (women)

**Division II:**
- Basketball: 10 scholarships (men), 10 (women)
- Football: 36 scholarships
- Baseball: 9 scholarships
- Track & Field: 12.6 (men), 12.6 (women)
- Soccer: 9 (men), 9.9 (women)

**Division III:**
- No athletic scholarships offered
- Focus on academic scholarships and need-based aid
- Merit-based awards available
- Work-study and grant opportunities
- Often comparable total aid to D1/D2 partial scholarships

**NAIA:**
- Basketball: 8 scholarships (men), 8 (women)
- Football: 24 scholarships
- Baseball: 12 scholarships
- Track & Field: 12 (men), 12 (women)
- More flexible distribution rules than NCAA

**JUCO:**
- Basketball: 15 scholarships (men), 15 (women)
- Football: 85 scholarships
- Baseball: 24 scholarships
- Typically limited to tuition, fees, and books
- Housing and meals are often not included

**The Reality of Athletic Aid**
**Average Scholarship Values:**
- D1 men's basketball (non-starter): $8,000-$15,000 annually
- D1 women's basketball (non-starter): $10,000-$20,000 annually
- D1 Olympic sports: $5,000-$15,000 annually
- D2 partial scholarships: $4,000-$10,000 annually
- NAIA scholarships: $5,000-$12,000 annually

**Hidden Costs of College Athletics:**
- Summer session expenses (often not covered)
- Training gear and equipment
- Nutritional supplements
- Travel home during breaks
- Social activities and personal expenses

**Scholarship Security Concerns:**
- Annual renewal (not guaranteed four years)
- Performance expectations
- Injury risks and medical coverage
- Coaching changes impact
- Transfer implications and restrictions

## LESSON 2: NEGOTIATING SCHOLARSHIP OFFERS
### Evaluating Offers Beyond the Money

**Program Fit Assessment:**
- Playing time opportunities
- Coaching staff stability
- Team culture and values alignment
- Development history of similar players
- Professional pathway potential

**Academic Considerations:**
- Strength of degree program
- Academic support services
- Graduation rates for athletes
- Career placement success
- Internship and networking opportunities

**Quality of Life Factors:**
- Campus environment and culture
- Distance from home
- Climate and geographic preferences
- Housing quality and meal plans
- Social and recreational opportunities

**Long-Term Planning:**
- Professional sports probability
- Career preparation beyond athletics
- Alumni network strength
- Graduate school opportunities
- NIL potential at the institution

### Leverage Points in Negotiations

**Multiple Offer Strategy:**
- Maintaining relationships with several programs
- Transparent communication about other interest
- Understanding each program's timeline
- Using competing offers appropriately
- Avoiding commitment until ready

**Performance Leverage:**
- Continued skill development during recruitment
- Showcase performances after initial offers
- Statistical improvements in key areas
- Physical development and measurables
- Awards and recognition achievements

**Academic Leverage:**
- Strong GPA for academic scholarships
- Test score improvements
- AP/IB course completion
- Academic honors and achievements
- Demonstration of time management skills

**Timing Considerations:**
- Understanding program recruiting cycles
- Awareness of scholarship availability
- Early signing period versus regular period
- Walk-on with potential later scholarship
- Transfer portal timing as leverage

## Scholarship Negotiation Conversations

**Initial Offer Response:**
"Thank you for the offer, Coach. I'm genuinely excited about the opportunity to join your program. This is a major decision for my athletic and academic future, so I'd like to discuss a few aspects of the offer to ensure it's the best fit for both of us. Would you be open to continuing the conversation about how we can make this work optimally?"

**Requesting Improvement:**
"I've received another offer that includes [specific benefit]. While I'm extremely interested in your program because [specific reasons], the financial aspect is important for my family. Is there any flexibility in your offer or additional academic scholarships I might qualify for to help bridge the gap?"

**Addressing Playing Time Concerns:**
"I believe I can contribute significantly to the program, and I'm wondering if you could share your vision for my role on the team, particularly regarding development and playing time expectations over my four years."

**Commitment Timeline Discussion:**
"I'm very interested in your program, but I'm still in discussions with a few other schools. Could you help me understand your timeline for a decision and what the next steps would be if I were to commit to your program?"

**Finalizing Your Decision**
**Decision Matrix Creation:**
- List all schools with offers
- Create weighted categories:
Athletic fit (30%)
Academic quality (25%)
Financial package (20%)
Location/environment (15%)
Coaching relationship (10%)
- Score each school in each category (1-10)
- Calculate weighted totals

**Final Campus Visit:**
- Meeting with current players without coaches
- Experience typical daily schedule
- Attend classes in your potential major
- Stay overnight in student housing
- Meet with academic advisors

**Commitment Process:**
- Verbal commitment communication
- National Letter of Intent signing (if applicable)
- Scholarship agreement review and signing
- Housing and enrollment deposits
- Academic and athletic paperwork completion

**Declining Other Offers Gracefully:**
"Coach [Name], I want to thank you sincerely for the opportunity to join your program. After careful consideration, I've decided to commit to [School]. This was an extremely difficult decision, and I have the utmost respect for you and your program. I'm grateful for the time and interest you've invested in my recruitment, and I wish you and your team all the best."

## Quick Check: Module 3- How to Land a Scholarship and Secure Offers

1. What's the difference between a full and partial scholarship?
2. Why is academic performance just as important as athletic ability?
3. What is "stacking aid" and how can it be used effectively?
4. What's one thing to avoid during this stage of the process?
5. Who are the gatekeepers in the scholarship process?
6. Why is following up crucial once an offer is made?

## MODULE 4: THE NIL PLAYBOOK – EARNING MONEY BEFORE COLLEGE

### LESSON 1: UNDERSTANDING NIL (NAME, IMAGE, LIKENESS)
**NIL Fundamentals**

**What Is NIL?**
- Legal right to monetize your name, image, and likeness
- Revolutionary change to amateurism rules
- Varies by state and institution
- Opportunity to build business while competing
- Professional development beyond athletics

**Current NIL Regulations:**
- NCAA policy framework
- State law variations
- School-specific guidelines
- Disclosure requirements
- Prohibited categories (gambling, alcohol, etc.)

**Common NIL Activities:**
- Social media endorsements
- Autograph sessions
- Personal appearances
- Merchandise sales
- Content creation
- Local business partnerships

**NIL Misconceptions:**
- Not automatic or guaranteed
- Requires entrepreneurial effort
- Most deals are modest ($50-$500)
- Major deals are rare and highly competitive
- Performance and exposure directly impact opportunities

**NIL for High School Athletes State**
**Eligibility Rules:**
- 30+ states now allow high school NIL
- Many states still prohibit it for maintaining eligibility
- School and district policies may differ
- Public vs. private school variations
- Ongoing legislative changes

**High School NIL Opportunities:**
- Local business partnerships
- Social media content creation
- Youth camps and clinics
- Merchandise and apparel
- Personal appearances in community

**Protecting Future Eligibility:**
- Research state and school policies thoroughly
- Document all NIL activities
- Maintain clear separation from recruiting
- Avoid professional representation conflicts
- Regular communication with school administration

**College Recruitment Impact:**
- NIL potential as recruiting factor
- School support infrastructure comparison
- Market size and opportunity differences
- Coach attitudes toward NIL activities
- Balancing time demands with athletics/academics

## LESSON 2: BUILDING YOUR PERSONAL BRAND
### Personal Brand Foundations

**Brand Identity Development:**
- Define your unique value proposition
- Identify personal strengths and attributes
- Establish core values and principles
- Create consistent visual elements
- Develop authentic voice and messaging

**Target Audience Identification:**
- Local community and businesses
- Sports-specific fans and followers
- Peer athletes and youth participants
- Industry-related companies
- Cause-related organizations

**Content Pillars:**
- Athletic performance and training
- Behind-the-scenes/day-in-the-life
- Personal interests and hobbies
- Community involvement
- Educational journey

**Brand Storytelling:**
- Personal journey narrative
- Obstacles overcome
- Motivations and inspirations
- Future goals and aspirations
- Community connections

### Social Media Strategy

**Platform Selection:**
- Instagram: Visual journey and highlights
- Twitter: Quick updates and engagement
- TikTok: Personality and entertainment
- YouTube: Long-form content and tutorials
- LinkedIn: Professional development and networking

**Content Calendar Creation:**
- Consistent posting schedule
- Batch content creation approach
- Special event planning
- Season vs. off-season strategies

**Engagement Techniques:**
- Authentic community interaction
- Strategic hashtag usage
- Collaboration with teammates
- Q&A and interactive features
- Responding to comments and messages

**Analytics and Optimization:**
- Key performance indicators tracking
- Content performance analysis
- Audience growth measurement
- Engagement rate monitoring
- Content strategy adjustments

## Monetization Strategies

**Direct Partnership Approach:**
- Local business identification
- Value proposition preparation
- Meeting request email templates
- Proposal and rate card development
- Contract negotiation basics

**Passive Income Streams:**
- Merchandise development and sales
- Digital product creation
- Affiliate marketing opportunities
- Platform monetization (YouTube, etc.)
- Subscription content models

**Service-Based Offerings:**
- Individual training sessions
- Camps and clinics
- Speaking engagements
- Appearances and autographs
- Coaching and mentorship

**Content Monetization:**
- Sponsored posts and content
- Product reviews and demonstrations
- Platform-specific monetization
- Brand ambassador programs
- Content licensing opportunities

## LESSON 3: EXECUTING NIL DEALS
### Finding NIL Opportunities

**Proactive Outreach Strategies:**
- Local business research and targeting
- Cold email and social media outreach
- Networking at community events
- Alumni and booster connections
- Industry-specific brand identification

**Marketplace Platforms:**
- Opendorse, INFLCR, Dreamfield
- Match Point Connection, Postgame
- Athlete marketplace registration
- Profile optimization for discovery
- Deal evaluation and acceptance

**Agent and Representative Considerations:**
- NCAA and state regulations
- Marketing vs. contract representation
- Fee structures and expectations
- Service evaluation criteria
- Risk/benefit assessment

**School Resources:**
- NIL education and training programs
- Compliance office guidance
- Business school partnerships
- Alumni network connections
- Legal and tax support services

### NIL Deal Valuation
**Market Rate Factors:**
- Sport and position played
- Social media following and engagement
- Content quality and production value
- Geographic market size
- Competition level and visibility

**Deal Structure Types:**
- Flat fee arrangements
- Performance-based incentives
- Royalty and revenue share models
- Product-for-post exchanges
- Long-term ambassador programs

**Value-Based Pricing:**
- Hourly rate calculations
- Deliverable-based pricing
- Exposure and impression metrics
- Engagement rate valuation
- Comparison to professional rates

**Negotiation Fundamentals:**
- Initial offer response strategies
- Value-add proposition development
- Multiple deal leverage
- Walking away principles
- Long-term relationship focus

**Legal and Tax Considerations**

**Contract Essentials:**
- Scope of work specification
- Compensation terms and timing
- Exclusivity provisions
- Content usage rights
- Term length and termination

**Tax Obligations:**
- Self-employment tax basics
- Quarterly estimated payments
- Expense tracking and deductions
- State tax considerations
- Business entity decisions

**Compliance Requirements:**
- School disclosure procedures
- NCAA reporting standards
- State law compliance
- Prohibited categories and activities
- Conflict of interest management

**Protecting Your Rights:**
- Intellectual property basics
- Image and content ownership
- Contract review best practices
- Red flags in agreements
- Dispute resolution mechanisms

**NIL Success Case Studies**

**Case Study: Local Business Partnership** *High School Basketball Player, Small Town USA*
- Identified local sporting goods store
- Proposed Instagram partnership (2 posts/month)
- Negotiated $150/month plus free gear
- Drove 15% traffic increase to store
- Built long-term relationship spanning college career

**Case Study: Content Creator** *Volleyball Player, Large Metropolitan Area*
- Developed technical training YouTube channel
- Grew to 50,000 subscribers in one year
- Attracted equipment sponsor at $500/video
- Created digital training program ($15,000 revenue)
- Leveraged following for college recruitment advantage

**Case Study: Group NIL Venture** *Football Team, Midwest High School*
- Entire offensive line created BBQ sauce brand
- Secured local manufacturing partnership
- Generated $20,000 in first-year sales
- Split revenue among team members
- Expanded to regional distribution during college

**Case Study: Camp Entrepreneur** *Soccer Player, Southern California*
- Launched youth skills camp during summer
- Charged $200 per participant (30 attendees)
- Secured facility through high school connection
- Partnered with local business for sponsorship
- Created recurring revenue stream through quarterly events

**Quick Check: Module 4- The NIL Playbook**
1. What does NIL stand for and why does it matter before college?
2. What's one example of a legal way to earn NIL money?
3. What are two common mistakes young athletes make when managing NIL deals?
4. How does your social media presence affect NIL opportunities?
5. Why should families be cautious when signing with agents or brands?
6. What role does understanding state law play in NIL compliance?

## MODULE 5: THE FINAL RECRUITING ACTION PLAN
## LESSON 1: BUILDING YOUR RECRUITING TIMELINE

**Freshman Year Action Plan (9th Grade)**

**Academic Focus:**
- Establish strong GPA foundation (3.5+ target)
- Select college preparatory courses
- Develop study habits and time management
- Research NCAA core course requirements
- Begin standardized test preparation

**Athletic Development:**
- Fundamental skill development priority
- Physical training foundation building
- Multiple sport participation benefits
- Position-specific training introduction
- Game film baseline establishment

**Research Phase:**
- Understand divisions and levels
- Create initial college interest list
- Research academic programs
- Attending college games if possible
- Begin understanding financial requirements

**Relationship Building:**
- Connect with high school coaches
- Explore AAU/club team options
- Meet with academic counselors
- Attend local camps and clinics
- Begin following college programs of interest

**Sophomore Year Action Plan (10th Grade) Academic Advancement:**
- Maintain/improve GPA (3.5+ target)
- Select appropriate AP/Honors courses
- Take PSAT/Pre-ACT exams
- Register with NCAA Eligibility Center
- Research academic interests and potential majors

**Athletic Progression:**
- Seek varsity playing time
- Join competitive AAU/club program
- Attend skill-specific camps
- Begin creating highlight videos
- Identify athletic strengths and weaknesses

**Exposure Opportunities:**
- Attend college camps selectively
- Competing in visible tournaments
- Begin social media presence building
- Create recruiting profiles on platforms
- Attend showcases appropriate for level

**Initial Outreach:**
- Research 20-30 schools of interest
- Create contact management system
- Develop initial introduction email
- Begin following college coaches on social media
- Prepare questions for potential coach conversations

**Junior Year Action Plan (11th Grade) Academic Acceleration:**
- Maintain strong GPA in challenging courses
- Take SAT/ACT exams (multiple if needed)
- Ensure NCAA core course progression
- Research specific academic programs
- Begin college application preparation

**Athletic Showcasing:**
- Varsity leadership role development
- High-level AAU/club participation
- Position-specific showcases attendance
- Updated highlight video creation
- Game film collection and organization

**Recruitment Intensification:**
- Targeted coach outreach campaign
- Showcase and tournament participation
- Unofficial campus visits scheduling
- Conversations with current college athletes
- Social media presence optimization

### Offer Management:
- Begin receiving and evaluating interest
- Unofficial visit planning and execution
- Understand scholarship possibilities
- Develop comparison metrics
- Narrow school list to realistic options

## Senior Year Action Plan (12th Grade)

### Academic Completion:
- Maintain GPA through graduation
- Complete NCAA core course requirements
- Final SAT/ACT attempts if needed
- College application submission
- Scholarship application completion

### Athletic Finalization:
- Varsity leadership demonstration
- Final highlight video update
- Select showcases for undecided athletes
- Physical development continuation
- Injury prevention focus

### Recruitment Decision:
- Official visit scheduling and completion
- Final school list narrowing (3-5 schools)
- Scholarship and aid package comparison
- Program fit final evaluation
- Decision timeline establishment

### Commitment Process:
- Verbal commitment communication
- National Letter of Intent signing
- Scholarship agreement review
- Housing and enrollment deposits
- Academic and athletic paperwork completion

## LESSON 2: ESSENTIAL RECRUITING TOOLS AND RESOURCES
### Contact Management System

**Coach Contact Database:**
- Name, position, school
- Contact information
- Communication history
- Specific interests noted
- Follow-up schedule

**School Tracking Matrix:**
- Academic fit rating
- Athletic opportunity rating
- Financial package details
- Location/environment notes
- Overall ranking system

**Communication Calendar:**
- Regular outreach schedule
- Tournament follow-up reminders
- Campus visits planning
- Application deadlines
- Decision timeline

**Resource Links Library:**
- NCAA eligibility resources
- School-specific information
- Recruiting platform profiles
- Highlight video access
- Academic transcripts and test scores

### Video and Media Assets
**Highlight Video Requirements:**
- 3-5 minutes maximum length
- Clear player identification
- Game footage (not practice)
- Skills demonstration sequence
- Contact information overlays

**Game Film Organization:**
- Complete game footage library
- Key games against quality competition
- Organized by date and opponent
- Accessible online platform that is easily shareable with coaches

**Academic and Character Evidence:**
- Community service documentation
- Academic achievements and awards
- Leadership roles and responsibilities
- Character reference letters
- Classroom and study evidence

**Digital Portfolio Components:**
- Athletic achievements section
- Academic credentials page
- Personal statement video
- Coach and character references
- Contact information and links

## Financial Planning Resources

**Scholarship Tracking Tool:**
- Athletic scholarship offers
- Academic scholarship opportunities
- Need-based aid eligibility
- Federal and state grants
- Total cost comparison worksheet

**College Cost Calculator:**
- Tuition, fees, room, and board
- Books and supplies estimates
- Travel expenses projection
- Personal expenses budget
- Athletic-specific costs

**Financial Aid Application Timeline:**
- FAFSA submission deadlines
- CSS Profile requirements
- Institutional aid applications
- Scholarship application calendar
- Award acceptance deadlines

**NIL Income Planning:**
- Projected NIL opportunities
- Tax obligation calculations
- Business expense tracking
- Investment and savings strategies
- Financial advisor considerations

## Legal and Compliance Tools

**NCAA Eligibility Checklist:**
- Core course completion tracking
- GPA calculation worksheet
- Test score requirements
- Amateurism certification steps
- International student requirements

**Recruiting Rules Reference:**
- Contact period guidelines
- Official vs. unofficial visit rules
- Communication regulations
- Financial aid limitations
- Signing period requirements

**Transfer Portal Guidelines:**
- Entry process and timing
- Eligibility implications
- Scholarship release requirements
- Contact rules for transfers
- Academic progress requirements

**NIL Compliance Toolkit:**
- State law summary
- School-specific guidelines
- Disclosure documentation
- Prohibited activities list
- Contract review checklist

## LESSON 3: BEYOND THE SCHOLARSHIP - COLLEGE SUCCESS

**Athletic Success Strategies First-Year**

**Transition Plan:**
- Summer preparation recommendations
- Preseason expectations management
- Training schedule adaptation
- Recovery protocol implementation
- Early playing time strategies

**Performance Development Path:**
- Position-specific improvement plans
- Strength and conditioning progression
- Film study and basketball IQ development
- Goal-setting framework
- Performance tracking methods

**Relationship Management:**
- Coach communication approach
- Teammate connection building
- Support staff utilization
- Conflict resolution strategies
- Leadership development pathway

**Professional Pathway Preparation:**
- Professional evaluation timeline
- Agent consideration process
- Overseas opportunity exploration
- Showcase and draft preparation
- Alternative career planning

**Academic Excellence Framework**

**Student-Athlete Support Utilization:**
- Academic advisor relationship
- Tutor and study hall resources
- Time management systems
- Professor communication strategies
- Travel accommodations

**Major and Career Planning:**
- Major selection guidelines
- Course scheduling strategies
- Internship and practical experience
- Networking with alumni
- Graduate school preparation

**Academic Recognition Opportunities:**
- Academic All-American requirements
- Conference honor roll standards
- Prestigious scholarship applications
- Academic honors societies
- Post-graduate award opportunities

**Balancing Athletics and Academics:**
- Weekly schedule development
- Priority management system
- Strategic course selection
- Communication with professors
- Using travel time effectively

## NIL Management in College

**School-Specific Program Integration:**
- Understanding institutional resources
- Compliance office relationship
- Marketplace platform access
- Team-specific guidelines
- Coach expectations management

**Time Management Strategies:**
- Scheduling NIL activities strategically
- Off-season focus for major projects
- In-season maintenance approach
- Calendar blocking for NIL work
- Setting clear boundaries with partners

**Performance-NIL Balance:**
- Athletic achievement always comes first
- Correlation between performance and NIL value
- Using NIL as motivation, not distraction
- Building on-field accomplishments into content
- Leveraging success for increased opportunities

**Team Dynamics Consideration:**
- Navigating jealousy or comparison
- Collaborative opportunities with teammates
- Supporting team-wide NIL initiatives
- Creating win-win situations
- Maintaining team culture and unity

**Brand Growth Throughout College:**
- Freshman to senior year evolution
- Building on each season's accomplishments
- Expanding reach and influence
- Developing industry relationships
- Creating sustainable post-graduation opportunities

## LESSON 4: LIFE AFTER COLLEGE ATHLETICS
### Career Transition Planning
**Professional Athletic Pursuits:**
- Realistic assessment of professional potential
- Agent selection and representation
- Pre-draft/combine preparation
- International playing opportunities
- League-specific preparation strategies

**Athletic-Adjacent Careers:**
- Coaching and player development
- Sports administration and management
- Athletic training and conditioning
- Sports media and communications
- Recreation and athletic directing

**Transferable Skills Identification:**
- Leadership and team collaboration
- Time management and discipline
- Performance under pressure
- Goal setting and achievement
- Resilience and adaptability

**Networking and Relationship Building:**
- Alumni association involvement
- Coach recommendation utilization
- Professional organization membership
- Industry-specific conferences
- Informational interview strategies

### Financial Literacy and Management
**College-to-Career Financial Transition:**
- Student loan management strategies
- First job budgeting and planning
- Housing and living expenses
- Tax implications post-graduation
- Credit building and management

**Athletic Earnings Management:**
- Professional contract structures
- Endorsement and sponsorship income
- Agent fees and representation costs
- Insurance considerations
- Retirement planning from day one

**NIL Income Integration:**
- Continuing NIL relationships post-college
- Building business based on NIL foundation
- Personal brand monetization long-term
- Content and media platform development
- Speaking and appearance opportunities

**Investment Fundamentals:**
- Long-term financial planning
- Retirement account types and benefits
- Investment options and risk profiles
- Real estate consideration
- Business ownership opportunities

**Mental Health and Identity Transition**

**Athletic Identity Evolution:**
- Transitioning from "athlete" as primary identity
- Finding purpose beyond competition
- Maintaining physical wellness post-career
- Developing new passion areas
- Building community outside of sports

**Psychological Adjustment Strategies:**
- Loss and grief processing
- New goal establishment
- Support system utilization
- Professional resources when needed
- Finding meaning in new challenges

**Physical Health Maintenance:**
- Injury management long-term
- Transitioning training approaches
- Nutrition adjustments post-competition
- Sustainable fitness practices
- Healthcare management strategies

**Creating Your Next Chapter:**
- Purpose discovery exercises
- Legacy consideration and development
- Mentorship opportunities (giving back)
- Continued personal growth commitment
- Life balance achievement strategies

**Quick Check: Module 5- The Final Recruiting Action Plan**
1. What are the final key steps every athlete should take?
2. Why is communication with coaches critical in the final stretch?
3. What's one way to evaluate if a program is the right fit?
4. What is one thing families often fail to do at the end of the recruiting process?
5. How can a backup plan help secure long-term success?
6. What's one takeaway from this module that will have a lasting impact?

## BONUS CONTENT: PARENT & COACH GUIDES
## PARENTS' GUIDE TO ATHLETIC RECRUITMENT

### Understanding Your Role
- Supporter vs. manager distinction
- When to step forward vs. step back
- Empowering athlete independence
- Financial and logistical contributions
- Emotional support strategies

### Communication Guidelines
- Parent-coach interaction best practices
- Parent-athlete productive conversations
- Questions to ask college coaches
- Red flags in recruitment process
- Navigating tough decisions together

### Financial Planning For Families
- Athletic scholarship reality check
- Educational funding alternatives
- Tournament and travel budgeting
- ROI consideration and analysis
- Long-term educational investment strategy

### Supporting Your Athlete's Journey
- Managing expectations realistically
- Handling disappointment and setbacks
- Celebrating achievements appropriately
- Balance and perspective maintenance
- Health and wellness priority enforcement

## COACHES' GUIDE TO SUPPORTING RECRUITMENT

### Program Development For Recruitment Success
- College coach relationship building
- Program reputation enhancement
- Showcase and tournament selection
- College pipeline establishment
- Success story documentation and promotion

**Individual Athlete Development**
- Realistic college level assessment
- Position-specific development plans
- Exposure opportunity creation
- Recommendation and advocacy
- Managing expectations with families

**Facilitating College Connections**
- College coach introduction protocols
- Campus visits coordination
- Reference and recommendation best practices
- Film and highlight sharing systems
- Recruitment event hosting

**Managing Team NIL Environment**
- Team culture preservation strategies
- Collaborative opportunity development
- Equity and fairness considerations
- Program-wide brand building
- Balancing individual and team interests

## CONCLUSION: YOUR RECRUITING SUCCESS ROADMAP
### Navigating Your Journey

**Immediate Next Steps**
- Current grade level starting points
- Priority assessment and planning
- Resource utilization strategy
- Support system activation
- First action items implementation

**Measuring Your Progress**
- Timeline checkpoint establishment
- Success indicator identification
- Course correction strategies
- Accomplishment documentation
- Regular reassessment protocols

**Community And Support**
- Joining our athlete community
- Mentor connection opportunities
- Peer networking benefits
- Parent support resources
- Ongoing education and updates

**Final Thoughts: The Bigger Picture**
- Athletics as life preparation
- Character and personal development
- Education as the ultimate goal
- Relationships and network building
- Finding joy in the journey

## Final Quiz Wrap-Up: What Did You Retain?

You've made it through the five modules, and each was packed with insight, real strategy, and a blueprint for action. Before you move into the next phase, take a moment to see what stuck. Use this as a self-check, or pass it to your team, your parents, or your players. It's not about passing or failing, it's about ***understanding what matters most.*** The questions that follow are designed to help you slow down, think critically, and assess whether you're ready to take the next step with confidence and clarity.

Final Quiz & Wrap Up
1. What are the three key stages of the college recruiting process?
2. How can an athlete stand out without a national ranking?
3. What role do parents play in helping athletes stay eligible and focused?
4. What does a good introductory message to a coach include?
5. What is one thing every athlete should know about scholarships?
6. How do NIL opportunities impact a student-athlete before they reach college?
7. What are two red flags to look out for in a recruiting offer?
8. What should every athlete be doing right now to prepare for recruitment?
9. Why is it dangerous to rely solely on exposure camps and showcases?
10. What does it really mean to "own your process"?

**Conclusion**

Everything that you've read up to this point was written with a clear purpose. It's not about theory, it's about how to move in real time, with tangible results. The recruiting process is layered, but it's not out of reach for those who understand how it works. This guide was created to remove the fog and give you something solid to work from whether you're an athlete, parent, or coach.

## JOURNALS & FOOD FOR THOUGHT

**The Billion-Dollar Pipeline: How Grassroots Basketball Became An Exploitation Machine**

The phone call always comes at dinner time. A coach with a warm voice and impressive credentials reaches out to a family whose 14-year-old son has been "identified" as special talent. The opportunity sounds incredible: elite competition, college exposure, potential scholarships. All for a modest investment of $3,000 for the summer season.

What the coach doesn't mention is that this phone call represents the entry point into America's most sophisticated system for extracting wealth from families while treating children as commodities in a $15 billion youth sports industry. Behind the promise of athletic scholarships and NBA dreams lies a financial network so complex that even seasoned investigators struggle to trace where the money goes. This is the business of grassroots basketball, where corporate giants, tournament operators, and coaches have created an exploitation machine that systematically harvests resources from families while enriching everyone except the athletes it claims to serve.

**The Financial Web**

The Amateur Athletic Union, founded in 1888 to promote youth sports, now oversees an empire that would make Wall Street executives envious. Some tournament operators who have generated over $20 million annually, have perfected the art of financial obfuscation. Consider the economics of a single major tournament. Entry fees of $10,000 per team across 50 teams in five states generate $2.5 million. Sponsor fees of $30,000 each from 30 companies per state add another $4.5 million. College coaches pay $5,000-$10,000 for "VIP access," contributing an additional $2.25 million. The total: nearly $8 million in revenue for a single weekend event. But this is merely the surface layer. Below lies a labyrinth of Limited Liability Companies and shell corporations designed to obscure money flows. Multiple entities with names like "Youth Development," "Athletic Marketing," and "Sports Consulting" create layers of separation between original funding sources and final recipients.

Each entity plays a role in moving money through the system. Sponsorship dollars from major shoe companies might start at one marketing company, transfer to another for "event planning services," move to a third for "talent development," before reaching families as "consulting fees" for vague services like "community outreach."

The amounts are staggering. Families pay between $400 and $4,000 per summer for AAU participation, not including travel, lodging, and meals that can easily double those costs. Private sport clubs represent a $15 billion industry, with 63% of parents paying $1,200-$6,000 annually for their children's participation.

## The Human Cost

Twelve-year-old Andre practices alone on a Detroit court when a coach approaches with an offer that changes everything. The man promises new sneakers, tournament opportunities, and a pathway to college scholarships. Andre's grandmother, raising three children on a fixed income, sees hope in her grandson's talent. What she doesn't understand is that Andre has become an asset in a complex financial equation. Within this world, children are viewed as commodities, an asset that could one day be worth hundreds of millions of dollars. The psychological manipulation begins immediately. Coaches create artificial scarcity, suggesting that opportunities are limited and must be seized quickly. They exploit parental love and economic anxiety, positioning basketball as the family's path to financial security.

The pattern repeats across the country with documented consequences. The 2017 FBI investigation revealed families receiving payments ranging from $5,000 to $100,000 in exchange for commitments to specific schools and shoe company relationships. When athletic careers end unexpectedly due to injury or other circumstances, young people who prioritized basketball over academics often find themselves without viable alternatives. Overuse injuries, burnout, and financial stress are all commonplace for both athletes and their families. Former NBA champion Robert Horry captured the dysfunction: "I hate AAU basketball. There's a lot of coaches that are exploiting these kids to try and get a payoff one day."

## Corporate Capture

The transformation of youth basketball into a corporate battlefield began in the 1990s when shoe companies recognized the marketing potential of young athletes. Companies like Nike and Adidas sponsor these players. They get them to wear their shoes and apparel and when their millions of followers see them, they will see the sneaker company too. The mechanism is elegant in its simplicity. Big time AAU leagues will find top players who play for unsponsored teams and give them cold hard cash to be used as a "travel budget" which of course is almost never used for travel.

The real currency is access to elite tournaments that coaches use to scout talent. Nike's Elite Youth Basketball League, Under Armour Association, and the Adidas Gauntlet function as parallel recruiting circuits. Nearly every American-born NBA player participated in AAU, making it "a prerequisite for college and professional basketball recruitment". This creates a monopoly: families must pay to access the only pathway to higher levels of basketball. The financial arrangements become increasingly sophisticated. The 2017 FBI investigation revealed that Adidas executives paid at least $90,000 to families, with coaches accepting $5,000-$50,000 bribes to steer players toward specific universities and shoe company relationships.

## The Institutional Framework

The current system exists because legitimate institutions create the conditions that make exploitation profitable. NCAA eligibility rules that prevent direct payment to athletes' force money underground and through third party payment providers. High school transfer policies that prioritize athletics over academics incentivize families to chase better opportunities. College recruitment timelines that begin in middle school create artificial urgency.

Since 2015, the U.S. Attorney's Office for the Southern District of New York and the FBI have been investigating the criminal influence of money on coaches and student-athletes. Their findings revealed systematic corruption: coaches accepting cash bribes to influence players' decisions about financial advisors, agents paying families to secure future representation rights, and shoe companies funding payments to ensure athletes attended sponsored universities.

The 2018 trials exposed the mechanics of corruption. Financial advisor Marty Blazer, working as an FBI informant, documented how coaches would accept $50,000 bribes in exchange for steering players toward specific advisors. The money was structured to appear legitimate by listing consulting fees, travel reimbursements, and summer camp payments, but functioned as straightforward bribes. Even more troubling was the discovery that many coaches and administrators were unaware of the full scope of the financial networks operating around their programs. The complexity of the money flows created plausible deniability while ensuring that corruption could flourish.

## The New Corruption

As federal investigations concluded, the system adapted. Recent federal investigations are now targeting point-shaving operations and are described as "national in scope" involving multiple players and programs. The corruption has evolved from payment schemes to direct game manipulation. Investigators have identified unusual betting activity involving at least three college programs: North Carolina A&T, Mississippi Valley State, and Eastern Michigan. This pattern suggests that financial pressure on athletes has created new vulnerabilities to criminal exploitation. The gambling investigations reveal how the grassroots system creates conditions for continued corruption. Players who received financial support throughout their youth careers arrive at college with compromised integrity and ongoing financial pressures. When legitimate opportunities for compensation remain limited, they become susceptible to offers from gambling operations.

## The International Perspective

While American basketball drowns in corruption and commercialization, international programs focus on development and education. The last seven NBA MVPs have all been foreign-born, suggesting that the American model is failing even by its own metrics. European basketball academies emphasize skill development over showcase competitions. Players attend school in the morning, practice in the afternoon, and compete in meaningful games on weekends. The focus remains on long-term development rather than immediate exposure. Nikola Jokić and Luka Dončić are examples of players that developed through systems that prioritized balance over intensity. They spend many of their offseason visiting family and pursuing interests outside basketball. This approach produces not only better players but more well-rounded individuals.

The contrast is stark. American players arrive at professional levels with overuse injuries, academic deficiencies, and psychological burnout. Their international counterparts often speak multiple languages, understand complex tactical systems, and demonstrate emotional maturity that comes from balanced development.

## The Economic Reality

The financial promises that drive family participation in grassroots basketball rarely materialize. The likelihood of getting a D1 scholarship for high school basketball players is less than 1 percent. Even full scholarships, when they occur, often fail to cover the total cost of college attendance. Meanwhile, families invest enormous resources chasing these minimal opportunities. A conservative estimate suggests that a family might spend $50,000-$100,000 over a child's youth career when including team fees, travel, equipment, training, and tournament costs. For most families, this represents a sizable portion of their wealth.

The economic disparity becomes self-perpetuating. In many places across the United States of America, it comes down to the haves and the have-nots. Families that can't afford AAU get left out in some respects and have to find other outlets for development. This creates a system where opportunity is increasingly restricted to affluent families, contradicting basketball's historical role as a pathway to social mobility for working-class communities.

## The Resistance

Some figures within the basketball community have begun speaking out against the current system. Former players who survived similar exploitation now work to protect the next generation of athletes. These advocates experienced firsthand how institutional corruption operates within college programs. They witnessed the complex financial networks that extract value from young talent while providing minimal protection or genuine opportunity. Their approach focuses on education rather than prohibition.

Dr. Sarah Mitchell documents how the current system creates long-term psychological damage. "We're seeing athletes arrive at college with anxiety disorders, depression, and identity issues rooted in years of being treated as commodities," she explains. Attorney James Patterson, who specializes in sports law, provides legal services to families facing exploitation. His practice has handled dozens of cases where families discovered that tournament fees, travel expenses, and equipment costs were being marked up significantly beyond actual values. Sports journalist Maria Rodriguez has spent the last five years documenting abuses within the grassroots system. Her investigative series exposed how certain AAU programs functioned as money laundering operations, using youth basketball as cover for moving funds between shoe companies and college programs. Their collective message is clear: "The machinery of exploitation hasn't changed; it has simply become more sophisticated."

**Conclusion**

You can still practice alone on the court, but now at least you understand what the coach's offer can really mean. Only time will tell what side of the moral line the coach falls on. Through the intervention of advocates who experienced similar manipulation, families can learn to ask different questions: Who profits from this arrangement? What are the hidden costs? What alternatives exist? Even if you don't say the quiet part out loud, you can still strategize and produce a plan that can somewhat protect you as you go through the process.

The grassroots basketball exploitation machine depends on information asymmetry. Many families enter the system without understanding its financial mechanics or true costs. Too many make decisions based on promises rather than evidence and hope rather than analysis. The solution is not to destroy youth basketball but to restore its original purpose: providing young people with opportunities to develop skills, build character, and pursue education through athletic participation.

This requires dismantling the financial networks that treat children as commodities and rebuilding systems that serve athletes rather than exploiting them. The choice is clear: continue enabling a system that enriches adults while harvesting resources from families or demand fundamental changes that return youth basketball to its educational and developmental mission. The young people practicing on courts across America deserve better than to become assets in someone else's financial scheme. They deserve systems designed to help them flourish as students, athletes, and human beings. The question is whether the adults who control these systems have the courage to prioritize children's wellbeing over their own monetary interests. The answer will determine whether basketball remains a pathway to opportunity or continues its transformation into America's most sophisticated youth exploitation machine.

## The Real College Recruitment Game: What Families Don't Know

Families entering the college recruitment process are walking into a system designed to exploit their dreams while protecting institutional interests. Most families' approach college recruitment believing that academic achievement and athletic talent will be fairly evaluated by institutions committed to developing young people. This naive trust leaves them vulnerable to systematic deception that can destroy years of preparation and sacrifice in a matter of weeks.

The reality is that college recruitment, particularly in high-revenue sports, operates more like a financial market than an educational system. Students are commodities whose value fluctuates based on performance, publicity, and institutional needs that have nothing to do with individual merit or potential. In our novel, *For The Love of The Game*, when Malik, Elijah, and Clifford choose Georgetown University, they believe they're selecting an institution based on academic reputation, basketball program quality, and the opportunity to compete together. What they don't realize is that they're entering a system where their scholarships, playing time, and even eligibility can disappear overnight due to decisions made by adults they've never met. The Georgetown investigation reveals payments to previous players, shadowy financial arrangements between coaches and recruiting services, and institutional knowledge of rule violations that reaches the highest levels of university administration. Yet the current players who benefited from none of these arrangements and knew nothing about the violations face consequences that could derail their academic and athletic futures.

This pattern repeats across college athletics with depressing regularity. Institutions violate rules to gain competitive advantages, generate millions in revenue from increased visibility and success, then sacrifice current students when investigations threaten those revenue streams. Understanding how this system actually works requires looking beyond official recruitment presentations to the financial incentives driving institutional behavior.

## The Economics of College Recruitment

Major college sports programs generate enormous revenue through television contracts, ticket sales, merchandise, and alumni donations tied to team success. A successful basketball program can generate $20-50 million annually for a university; football programs can exceed $100 million. These revenue streams create pressure to win that corrupts every aspect of the recruitment process. Coaches' contracts include performance bonuses tied to tournament appearances and rankings; their job security depends on producing results that require recruiting the best available talent by any means necessary.

University administrators claim to value academic integrity while implementing policies that prioritize athletic revenue over educational mission. They hire coaches who promise results, provide minimal oversight of recruitment practices, then express shock when violations are discovered. The NCAA enforcement system enables this hypocrisy by imposing penalties that rarely threaten the fundamental revenue-generating capacity of major programs. Scholarships get reduced, tournament participation gets suspended, but television contracts and donor relationships remain intact. Meanwhile, student-athletes bear the primary consequences of institutional decisions they had no role in making. They lose scholarships, eligibility, and opportunities while the adults who created the violations often move to other programs with minimal career consequences.

**Red Flags Families Miss**

Most families focus on obvious recruitment benefits like scholarship offers, coaching promises, and facility quality, while missing warning signs that indicate institutional instability or ethical problems. Excessive recruiting pressure should raise immediate concerns. When coaches make repeated contact, offer unusually generous terms, or pressure families to commit quickly, these behaviors often indicate desperation that suggests underlying program problems.

Financial arrangements that seem too good to be true usually are. When families receive unexpected financial support for travel, equipment, or living expenses from sources connected to a program, these arrangements may violate rules in ways that could later jeopardize student eligibility. Coaching staff turnover provides crucial information about program stability. When assistant coaches leave frequently or head coaches change programs unexpectedly, families should investigate the reasons rather than assuming these changes don't affect current commitments.

Academic support that seems disconnected from legitimate educational goals indicates institutional priorities that may not serve student interests. When universities offer academic programs specifically designed for athletes, provide excessive tutoring support, or show flexibility about academic standards, these accommodations may create eligibility problems later.

**Financial Transparency**

How is the athletic department funded, and what percentage of revenue comes from the sport you're being recruited for? Programs heavily dependent on revenue from a single sport face pressure that affects every decision about scholarships, coaching, and rule compliance. What happens to scholarship commitments if coaching staff changes, program sanctions occur, or athletic department budget cuts become necessary? Many families discover too late that scholarship commitments are not guaranteed and can be reduced or eliminated for reasons beyond student control.

**Academic Integration**

How do student-athletes in your sport perform academically compared to general student population? Large disparities indicate that the program may not provide adequate support for genuine educational achievement. What percentage of student-athletes in your sport graduate within six years, and what types of degrees do they typically pursue? Programs that guide athletes toward less rigorous academic paths may not prepare them for post athletic careers.

## Compliance History

Has the program faced NCAA investigations or sanctions within the past ten years, and what were the specific violations? Past violations indicate institutional culture and compliance systems that may affect current students. How does the compliance office monitor recruiting activities, and what training coaches receive about current regulations? Weak compliance systems increase the risk of future violations that could affect current student-athletes.

## Protecting Your Interests

Families must approach college recruitment as a business negotiation rather than an academic evaluation. This means maintaining skepticism about institutional promises while documenting all commitments in writing.

## Independent Legal Review

Any family whose child receives significant scholarship offers should consult an attorney experienced in college athletics before signing commitments. The legal language in scholarship agreements often contains provisions that families don't understand until problems arise.

## Financial Backup Planning

Because athletic scholarships can be reduced or eliminated for several reasons, families should develop financial plans that don't depend entirely on institutional support. This includes understanding academic scholarship opportunities, federal financial aid eligibility, and family resources for continuing education if athletic support disappears.

## Academic Preparation

Student-athletes should prepare academically for the possibility that athletic careers will end earlier than expected due to injury, performance issues, or program changes. This means choosing academic programs based on genuine interest and career potential rather than ease or accommodation.

## Network Development

Building relationships with faculty, administrators, and professionals outside the athletic department provides alternative support systems if athletic programs face disruptions. Many student-athletes discover too late that their entire university experience was contained within athletic department relationships. The Georgetown scandal in our book demonstrates how quickly institutional support can evaporate when external pressures threaten program interests. Students who seemed secure in their positions suddenly face uncertainty about scholarships, eligibility, and academic standing through no fault of their own. But the scandal also reveals the importance of authentic relationships that transcend institutional arrangements. Malik, Elijah, and Clifford support each other through the crisis because their bond is based on mutual respect rather than shared benefit from a system that never really served their interests.

## Institutional vs. Personal Relationships

The most successful student-athletes build relationships with coaches, teammates, and university staff as individuals rather than just as representatives of institutions. When programs face disruptions, these personal relationships often provide support that institutional commitments cannot guarantee. This doesn't mean becoming emotionally dependent on coaches or athletic department staff; it means developing mutual respect and genuine care that survives changes in institutional circumstances. Similarly, athletes who build academic relationships outside the athletic department create alternative pathways for success that don't depend on athletic performance or program stability.

## The Current System's Future

College athletics is undergoing fundamental changes that will affect recruitment for years to come. Name, Image, and Likeness (NIL) rules are creating new revenue opportunities for student-athletes while also introducing new complexities around compliance and institutional control. Transfer portal policies are giving student-athletes more mobility while also increasing uncertainty about roster stability and scholarship security. Families entering recruitment today must understand that the college athletics landscape will continue evolving in ways that may affect four-year plans. These changes create both opportunities and risks that families must evaluate carefully. The same technological and regulatory developments that increase student-athlete leverage also create new ways for institutions to exploit information asymmetries and financial dependencies.

Ultimately, successful navigation of college recruitment requires understanding that institutions will always prioritize their own interests over individual student welfare when conflicts arise. This doesn't mean avoiding college athletics; it means entering the system with realistic expectations and comprehensive preparation for multiple scenarios. The families who succeed are those who treat college recruitment as one part of a broader educational and personal development strategy rather than as the single pathway to future success. They maintain perspective about athletic achievements while building the academic, social, and emotional foundation that will serve their children throughout their lives. Because in the end, the real college recruitment game isn't about finding the perfect program; it's about developing young people who can thrive regardless of which institutions they encounter or how those institutions treat them.

## Brotherhood Beyond Blood: What Young Men Really Need to Succeed

Young men today are starving for authentic connection while being fed a steady diet of toxic competition and hollow networking. For The Love of The Game has three types of brotherhood which are biological, chosen, and artistic. Each reveals what genuine support actually looks like when it's built on mutual respect rather than social media performance. Young men are told that success is an individual pursuit; that asking for help is weakness; that vulnerability compromises masculinity. These messages leave them isolated during the most crucial developmental years of their lives. The result is an epidemic of depression, anxiety, and suicide among young men who believe they must navigate life's complexities alone.

The characters in our book demonstrate a different model; one where strength comes through connection rather than isolation. Malik and Masterson represent biological brotherhood at its most powerful. They share DNA but more importantly, they share vision. Malik pursues basketball excellence while Masterson builds a hip-hop career through his group PHP, yet their different paths strengthen rather than divide their relationship. This isn't accidental. Many biological siblings become competitors rather than collaborators as they age, particularly when they're pursuing similar goals. Malik and Masterson avoid this trap by respecting each other's distinct talents and offering support that enhances rather than threatens individual achievement.

When Masterson's music career faces pressure from record labels trying to compromise his artistic integrity, Malik provides the kind of emotional support that money can't buy. He doesn't try to solve his brother's problems or give advice about an industry he doesn't understand; he simply reminds Masterson of his core values and his commitment to authentic expression. Similarly, when Malik faces the pressure of college recruitment and professional expectations, Masterson offers perspective that comes from understanding the entertainment industry's similar pressures. He helps Malik see that talent without integrity leads to hollow success, regardless of the field. This mutual support works because each brother recognizes that the other's success enhances rather than diminishes his own opportunities. Malik's athletic achievement opens doors for PHP's music; Masterson's artistic credibility gives Malik cultural authenticity that pure athletic success cannot provide.

Biological brotherhood requires intentional cultivation. DNA creates the potential for deep connection, but that potential only becomes reality when siblings choose to prioritize the relationship over individual advancement. Many young men lose their brothers to competition, resentment, or simple neglect during the years when brotherhood could provide the most value.

Malik, Elijah, and Clifford represent chosen brotherhood; the kind of connection that forms when young men recognize shared values and complementary strengths. Their bond develops through competition but deepens through mutual support during challenges that test character rather than skill. Their initial connection happens on the basketball court during an AAU tournament, but the relationship transcends sports from the beginning. They recognize in each other a commitment to excellence that goes beyond individual achievement. Each brings something essential that the others need. Malik's urban sophistication teaches Elijah and Clifford how to navigate social complexity with confidence rather than defensiveness. His understanding of cultural dynamics helps them avoid isolation when they encounter environments where their backgrounds might not be immediately understood or valued. Elijah's strategic thinking and risk assessment capabilities, developed through years of navigating genuine danger in Camden, help Malik and Clifford understand how to evaluate opportunities and threats with clarity rather than emotion. His ability to stay focused under pressure becomes invaluable when all three face the Georgetown scandal and other institutional challenges.

Clifford's intellectual curiosity and communication skills provide the group with analytical frameworks for understanding their experiences and planning their futures. His journalism instinct helps them to see beyond immediate pressures to long-term implications of their choices. But chosen brotherhood requires more than complementary skills, it requires emotional availability and mutual accountability that many young men avoid. Malik, Elijah, and Clifford learn to have conversations about fear, disappointment, and uncertainty without compromising their respect for each other's strength.

When Malik struggles with the decision to prioritize basketball over his relationship with Jasmine, his friends don't just offer platitudes about following his dreams. They help him think through the actual costs and benefits of his choice while supporting whatever decision he makes. This kind of emotional support requires maturity that many peer relationships never develop. When Elijah faces the crisis of his sister's legal troubles and must balance family obligations with team commitments, Malik and Clifford don't pressure him to choose sides. Instead, they help him find creative solutions that honor both obligations while offering practical support that makes those solutions possible.

**Biological brotherhood** can be cultivated by prioritizing family relationships even when individual paths diverge. This means regular communication that goes beyond surface-level updates; it means offering support that serves the other person's goals rather than your own preferences; it means celebrating others' success without comparing it to your own progress.

**Chosen brotherhood** develops through shared experiences that reveal character rather than just compatibility. Young men need opportunities to face meaningful challenges together; to support each other through failure as well as success; to have honest conversations about fear, ambition, and uncertainty without judgment or competition.

**Artistic or collaborative brotherhood** emerges when young men work together on projects that matter to all participants. This could be starting a business, organizing community service, creating artistic work, or building anything that requires sustained effort and shared vision. All three types of brotherhood require emotional skills that traditional masculine socialization often discourages. Young men must learn to be vulnerable without being needy; supportive without being controlling; competitive without being destructive; strong without being isolated.

The characters in our book demonstrate that these skills can be developed through practice and that the benefits extend far beyond individual relationships. Young men who master authentic brotherhood become better leaders, partners, fathers, and community members throughout their lives. They also become more resilient in the face of setbacks and more effective at achieving their individual goals. Contrary to cultural messages about self-reliance, the most successful young men are those who build the strongest support networks based on mutual respect and genuine care. Brotherhood isn't just nice to have; it's essential for male development and success. Young men who try to navigate life's complexities alone are fighting with one hand tied behind their backs. Those who build authentic brotherhood have access to collective wisdom, shared resources, and emotional support that make even the most challenging goals achievable. The question isn't whether young men need brotherhood; it's whether they'll have the courage to build it authentically or accept the hollow substitutes that culture offers instead.

## When Success Demands Sacrifice: Teaching Young People to Make Hard Choices

Young people today face impossible choices with inadequate preparation. We watch them navigate decisions that will shape their entire lives while adults offer platitudes instead of practical frameworks for moral reasoning under pressure. The three protagonists in our book each face moments where pursuing their dreams requires sacrificing something they value deeply. These aren't abstract ethical dilemmas from philosophy textbooks; these are the real choices that determine whether young people become who they want to be or who circumstances force them to be.

Malik's choice cuts to the core of modern relationships: can you love someone completely while pursuing a dream that demands everything? When his relationship with Jasmine reaches a breaking point, he's forced to choose between emotional fulfillment and professional focus. His decision to prioritize basketball over romance isn't callous; it's strategic thinking applied to matters of the heart. "I can't give up on my dreams," Malik tells Jasmine. "Basketball is everything to me right now." The honesty is brutal and necessary because he recognizes that half-hearted commitment to either relationship would serve neither well. The pain of his choice doesn't make it wrong. This reflects a broader challenge facing young people today: the mythology of "having it all" versus the reality of resource allocation. Time, energy, and focus are finite; excellence in any field requires concentration that inevitably means saying no to other opportunities. The adults who tell young people they can pursue every interest simultaneously are setting them up for mediocrity across the board.

Elijah's dilemma operates on a different level entirely. When his sister faces legal trouble and his family needs support, he must balance team obligations against family loyalty. Unlike Malik's choice between competing personal desires, Elijah faces competing moral obligations; his family needs him, but his teammates depend on him too. His solution demonstrates sophisticated ethical reasoning: he doesn't abandon either obligation but finds ways to fulfill both through careful time management and clear communication. He travels home when family crises demand it but maintains his commitment to the team when he's present; this approach requires more effort than choosing one over the other, but it preserves his integrity across both relationships. The lesson here isn't that you can always avoid hard choices through clever scheduling; sometimes you genuinely cannot serve multiple masters effectively. But before defaulting to either-or thinking, young people should exhaust the possibilities for creative solutions that honor competing commitments.

Clifford's journey reveals perhaps the most complex choice of all: how to develop multiple talents without diluting your impact. His passion for journalism grows alongside his basketball skills, creating tension between specialization and diversification; the conventional wisdom says, "pick one thing and become great at it." But Clifford discovers that combining different skills can create unique opportunities that pure specialization cannot access. His transition from player to sports journalist isn't abandoning basketball; it's leveraging his athletic experience to enhance his storytelling credibility. This represents strategic career thinking that recognizes how skills compound rather than compete when properly integrated. These character choices illuminate a decision-making framework that young people rarely receive explicitly.

**Clarify Your Non-Negotiables**
What values, relationships, or goals are you unwilling to sacrifice under any circumstances? Malik's basketball dreams, Elijah's family loyalty, Clifford's intellectual curiosity - these core commitments anchor their other decisions.

**Counting the Real Costs**
Every choice involves trade-offs, but many people focus only on what they're gaining while ignoring what they're losing. Malik's basketball focus costs him romantic intimacy; Elijah's family commitments cost him some team opportunities; Clifford's diverse interests cost him single-minded athletic development. Honest accounting prevents regretful surprises later.

**Consider Timing and Sequencing**
Not every choice is permanent. Malik's relationship sacrifice doesn't mean he'll never love again; it means he's not ready for that level of emotional investment while pursuing professional goals. Sometimes "not now" is more accurate than "never."

**Evaluate Your Support Systems**
Individual choices happen within relationship networks. Elijah can balance competing obligations partly because his family and teammates understand and support his attempts to honor both commitments. Weak support systems force harder choices than strong ones.

**Accept Responsibility for Outcomes**
Once you make a difficult choice, own it completely. Don't blame circumstances, other people, or bad luck for consequences you could anticipate. Malik doesn't resent basketball for costing him his relationship; he chose basketball knowing the price.

The current educational system fails young people by avoiding these conversations. We teach them to analyze literature, solve mathematical equations, and memorize historical facts, but we don't teach them how to reason through competing moral claims or evaluate long-term consequences of immediate decisions. This avoidance isn't accidental; adults prefer young people who defer difficult choices rather than making independent decisions that might challenge adult preferences. But postponing hard choices doesn't eliminate them; it just transfers decision-making power to circumstances and other people.

The characters in our book succeed not because they avoid difficult choices but because they develop frameworks for making those choices consciously rather than reactively. They learn to distinguish between choices that reflect their values and choices that compromise their integrity. This distinction matters enormously. Malik's choice to prioritize basketball reflects his deepest values about excellence and commitment; a choice to stay in the relationship while resenting the time it took from basketball would compromise his integrity toward both basketball and Jasmine. Sometimes the choice that feels hardest in the moment serves your integrity better than the choice that feels easier.

Young people also need to understand that moral courage often requires making choices that other people won't understand or support. Elijah's determination to support his family while maintaining team commitments might look like poor prioritization to people who don't understand his background. Clifford's interest in journalism might seem like distraction to coaches who want single-minded athletic focus. External criticism doesn't necessarily indicate poor decision-making. Sometimes it indicates that you're making choices based on your own values rather than other people's expectations. But this autonomy comes with a responsibility that many young people resist accepting full ownership of your choices and their consequences. You cannot maintain the integrity to make independent decisions while blaming other people when those decisions lead to outcomes you don't like.

The protagonists in our book mature when they stop looking for adults to make their hard choices for them and start developing their own capacity for moral reasoning under pressure. This doesn't mean ignoring advice or rejecting guidance. It means developing the judgment to evaluate advice against your own values and circumstances. This development process requires practice with progressively more consequential decisions. Young people need opportunities to make choices that matter, experience the outcomes, and refine their decision-making processes based on results. Protecting them from all difficult choices until they are adults leaves them unprepared for the complexity they'll inevitably face. The goal isn't to eliminate difficult choices from young people's lives. The goal is to prepare them to make those choices with integrity, wisdom, and acceptance of responsibility for outcomes. Because ultimately, the quality of your life depends not on avoiding hard choices but on making them in ways that reflect who you are and who you want to become.

## The Geography of Dreams: How Your Zip Code Shapes Your Future

Bobby May and I co-authored "For the Love of the Game" because we needed to show young people how geography shapes destiny in ways that most adults refuse to acknowledge. The three protagonists in our book, Malik from Harlem, Elijah from Camden, and Clifford from Canton, each carry the weight and advantages of their postal codes in every decision they make.

The numbers tell a story that goes beyond individual character or family values. Malik's Harlem neighborhood has a median household income of $37,073 with a 23% poverty rate. Elijah's Camden shows $26,105 median income with 36% poverty. Clifford's Canton sits at $31,838 with 25% poverty. These aren't just statistics; they're the economic foundation that determines everything from school quality to college preparation to the networks available for mentorship and opportunity. But the real impact of geography isn't captured in census data. It lives in the daily reality of what each location offers or denies to young people trying to build futures.

Malik's Harlem provides him with cultural richness that shapes his worldview in profound ways. He has access to Rucker Park, where basketball legends have played for generations; this isn't just a court, it's a classroom where he learns the history and artistry of his craft. The neighborhood's musical heritage flows through his family home via his brother Masterson's hip-hop production work. Malik grows up understanding that excellence has deep roots in his community. Yet even with these cultural advantages, Harlem's economic challenges create pressure that affects every decision. When Malik's family discusses college options, the conversation inevitably includes financial calculations that wealthier families never face. The question isn't just "which school offers the best opportunity" but "which school offers the best opportunity we can actually afford."

Elijah's Camden presents a starker reality. The violence that permeates his neighborhood isn't background noise; it's a daily factor in strategic thinking. When he walks to school or practice, route planning includes safety considerations that suburban kids never contemplate. The line "In Camden everything's a fight, Marcus. I'm just fighting mine with a ball instead of a gun" reflects the literal choice structure his environment creates. Camden's economic distress translates into limited institutional support for college preparation. The guidance counselors are overwhelmed, the library resources are outdated, and the network of professionals who could provide mentorship or internship opportunities is thin. Elijah's path to success requires navigating not just the normal challenges of adolescence but also the systematic disadvantages of his zip code imposes on his life.

Clifford's Canton represents the complexity of post-industrial America. The city carries the psychological weight of economic decline; it's a place where dreams historically went to die rather than flourish. Growing up as the son of a single mother in this environment means absorbing daily messages about limitation rather than possibility. Yet Canton's challenges also create certain advantages. The lower cost of living means Clifford's family can maintain housing stability that might be impossible in more expensive cities. The smaller scale of the community means individual achievement stands out more prominently; Clifford's talents don't get lost in the crowd the way they might in larger, more competitive environments. The geographic influence extends beyond economic factors to shape psychological development in ways that last long after these young men leave their hometowns.

Malik's Harlem experience teaches him to navigate cultural complexity and appreciate artistic excellence. He develops sophisticated social skills from growing up in a diverse, densely populated environment. These capabilities serve him well when he reaches Georgetown and later the NBA; he can code-switch between different social contexts with an ease that more sheltered backgrounds don't provide. Elijah's Camden experience forces him to develop strategic thinking and risk assessment capabilities that become valuable throughout his life. Learning to navigate genuine physical danger creates mental toughness and situational awareness that transfer to academic and professional challenges. His ability to stay focused under pressure, developed through years of managing real threats, becomes an asset in high-stakes basketball games and eventually in legal practice.

Clifford's Canton background instills a work ethic based on understanding that nothing gets handed to you. Growing up in a place where economic opportunity is scarce teaches him to maximize every advantage and waste nothing. This mentality drives his academic achievement and his eventual success in journalism; he approaches every opportunity with the intensity of someone who knows how rare they are. But geographic influence also creates blind spots and limitations that each character must overcome. Malik's urban sophistication sometimes translates into impatience with slower-paced environments or people who haven't experienced his level of cultural diversity. His assumption that everyone shares his urban worldview occasionally creates communication problems with teammates and coaches from diverse backgrounds. Elijah's survival-focused mindset, while valuable for handling genuine threats, sometimes leads him to perceive conflict where none exists. The defensive instincts that protect him in Camden can interfere with building trust in safer environments where vulnerability and openness would serve him better.

Clifford's scarcity mentality, while driving his work ethic, occasionally prevents him from taking risks that could lead to greater opportunities. The fear of losing what little he has can make him overly conservative in situations where bold action would produce better outcomes. Understanding these geographic influences becomes crucial for educational institutions, employers, and community organizations trying to serve young people effectively.

## Effective Support Systems

The characters in our book succeed not by denying their geographic origins but by understanding how those origins shape their strengths and limitations. They learn to leverage the advantages their backgrounds provide while developing skills to overcome the disadvantages. This approach requires honest assessment rather than either shame about limitations or romanticization of struggle. Geographic disadvantage is real and systematic; pretending it doesn't exist serves no one. But geographic background also creates resilience, creativity, and problem-solving capabilities that more privileged environments often fail to develop.

## Educational Implications

Schools serving students from economically disadvantaged areas must provide not just academic instruction but also cultural capital that suburban schools take for granted. This includes teaching students how to navigate institutional systems, build professional networks, and advocate for themselves in environments where their backgrounds might not be understood or valued. But schools serving more privileged students also need geographic diversity to prepare their students for the increasingly complex world they'll enter. Students who grow up in economic bubbles lack the problem-solving skills, cultural competence, and resilience that their peers from more challenging backgrounds develop naturally. The goal isn't to eliminate geographic influence on opportunity; that's neither possible nor necessarily desirable. Different environments create different strengths, and this diversity benefits society overall.

The goal is to ensure that geographic background doesn't create insurmountable barriers to achievement for young people with talent and determination. This requires systematic changes in how we structure educational opportunities, design support programs, and measure success. It also requires recognizing that the young people who overcome geographic disadvantages often bring exceptional capabilities that more privileged peers lack. Malik, Elijah, and Clifford each carry their neighborhoods with them throughout their journeys. They don't leave their zip codes behind when they achieve success; they transform their understanding of what those zip codes mean and what they make possible. Because ultimately, geography is destiny only when we accept that it has to be. When we understand how zip codes shape opportunity, we can design interventions that honor the strengths different environments create while removing the barriers that prevent talent from flourishing wherever it emerges.

## About The Authors

**C. Grooms** is a published author, educator, certified life coach, consultant who brings intellect, strategy, and lived experience to every space he enters. With academic training in Deviant Behavior and Social Control, Media and Communications, American Studies, and Sports Management, Grooms operates with both range and precision. His expertise allows him to speak to the realities of underserved communities, the pressure placed on young athletes, and the systemic gaps in education and leadership. He doesn't speculate. He educates, equips, and elevates.

He writes with clarity and conviction while also building platforms that blend cultural storytelling with community impact. His writing is layered with insight and driven by purpose. His coaching and consulting are rooted in results. Whether in print, in person, or behind the mic, he is committed to delivering content that moves people forward. He writes because the stories are real. He speaks because the message matters. He shows up because the next generation deserves more than recycled advice. They deserve the truth backed by proof. He is also a co-author of *For The Love of The Game* with Bobby May, a nonfiction novel based on real events and a teaching tool aimed at bringing cultural awareness and knowledge to its readers.

**Bobby May** spent over 20 years as a Catastrophe Claims Adjuster, helping individuals and families recover after some of life's most unexpected challenges. But his passion for serving others started long before that. His exceptional career began working as a staff member in group homes for juveniles. He saw firsthand the struggles many young people face without proper guidance and support. That experience inspired Bobby to open his own group homes, providing a safe space and structured environment for adolescents in need. Later, he worked as a Behavioral Specialist, helping youth navigate emotional and behavioral obstacles. These roles solidified his lifelong commitment to mentoring and uplifting the next generation.

Bobby May holds a Bachelor's degree in Criminal Justice with a concentration in Forensic Psychology and a Master's degree in Criminal Justice with an emphasis in Project Management. Today, he continues that mission through his work as a certified Life Coach, Business Consultant, and co-host of the Two Grumpy Men podcast, a platform where real talk meets life lessons and no topic is off-limits.

Whether Bobby is working with youth, coaching clients, or speaking from the mic, his goal remains the same: to help others unlock their potential, take control of their journey, and push forward no matter the obstacles. His motto is simple and personal: **Only the strong survive**. And true strength comes not just from what you've been through, but from what you're willing to rise above.

# Ultimate AAU & College Recruiting Playbook

## CHECK OUT THE NOVEL THAT INSPIRED THIS PLAYBOOK

GET THE NOVEL

PUBLISHER'S WEBSITE: TENGPUBLISHING.COM

INGRAMSPARK

AUTHOR'S WEBSITE: FORTHELOVEOFTHEGAME.XYZ

AMAZON

BOOKS.BY/AUTHORCGROOMS

www.ingramcontent.com/pod-product-compliance
Lightning Source LLC
Chambersburg PA
CBHW081127080526
44587CB00021B/3776